Video Game Addiction

How to End Your Video Game Addiction Once and For All

Table Of Contents

Introduction

Chapter 1: How to Tell When a Good Habit Goes Bad

Chapter 2: Turning Good Intentions into a Solid Plan

Chapter 3: The Slow and Steady Route

Chapter 4: Going Cold Turkey

Chapter 5: Staying Video Game Free for Life

Conclusion

Introduction

I want to thank you and congratulate you for downloading the book, Video Game Addiction – How to End Your Video Game Addiction Once and for All

This book contains proven steps and strategies on how to end your video game addiction.

As someone who used to be addicted to video games, I hope that the tips and strategies in this book will help you overcome this huge problem. They were effective for me, and I have every confidence they will work just as well for you.

Thanks again for downloading this book, I hope you enjoy it!

Chapter 1: How to Tell When a Good Habit Goes Bad

These days, everybody plays video games. New technology has made them more accessible than ever: even if you don't have a PlayStation or an Xbox 360 at home, you probably have games on your computer or your smart phone (even if it's only a simple puzzle game to help you pass the time during your daily commute). How many times have we been waiting at line and just pulled up Candy Crush to kill a few minutes?

Aside from the fact that they are simply good fun, there are a number of benefits that come from playing video games. Scientific studies have shown that they can improve hand-eye coordination and reaction time, and it is likely that they help with reasoning skills as well. Some games offer people opportunities to make new friends, and in many cases they offer a much-needed escape from the grind of daily life. However there is a dark side to this: it is possible to have too much of a good thing.

Video game addiction is a very real problem, and, while it may not be immediately life threatening, it needs to be addressed as the serious issue that it is. People who have suffered from it (or watched loved ones suffer) will not hesitate to classify it together with alcoholism, smoking and gambling. In fact, it is so significant and prevalent that the American Medical Association strongly encourages that 'video game addiction' be formally considered as a diagnostic mental disorder.
But how can you tell when you're hooked? When does your love for games turn into an addiction?

It Stops Being a Good When It Starts Being Disruptive

The rule of thumb here is that a fondness for video games becomes a full-blown addiction when it begins to disrupt your life. Binge gaming every other weekend is fine. Playing for half an hour or so every evening to help you unwind at the end of a long day is also all right. The problem starts when your need to play and your obsessive preoccupation with video games spill over and interfere with other aspects of your life.

Go through the following list and think hard about each item. If you show one or more of these signs, it is highly likely that you are suffering from a video game addiction:

1. You are extremely happy while playing video games, and get angry, irritable or depressed when you have to stop.

2. You constantly think about games even while you are doing other things.

3. You tend to neglect things like work or school requirements as long as you can go on playing – you simply don't find them as interesting or as important.

4. You spend more time playing than you do with your friends.

5. You need to spend longer amounts of time playing in order to feel satisfied.

6. You lie when people ask you how you spend your time on the computer or console.

7. You skip meals and neglect personal hygiene in order to keep playing for longer periods of time.

8. Your sleeping patterns become disrupted.

9. You dream about the game when you do get to sleep.

10. You spend a large amount of money on your games and game-related merchandise.

Try Looking at Your Behavior from a Different Point of View

Identifying a gaming addiction on your own can be tricky, however, and this can be a problem since addiction has to be acknowledged before it can be remedied. You are not always the best judge of your own behavior, and true video game addicts usually find ways to justify – at least to themselves – their compulsion to play.

Excuses such as 'I don't play nearly as much as some other people' and 'I won't be able to function if I don't get to play because video games are my happy place' often crop up in the face of blatant, problematic addiction, even when concerned friends and relatives do their best to point it out.

If you are having difficulty with the idea that you might be addicted to gaming, try and look at your behavior from a different point of view or an outside perspective. Let's say we're not talking about video games here: what would you think of someone who acted the same way about a TV or book series? If you would say that they need to ease up on their obsession, then so do you. The only thing that remains is for you to do something about it.

Chapter 2: Turning Good Intentions into a Solid Plan

When you recognize your video game addiction for what it is, it won't take you long to decide that something has to be done about it. It is easy to make the decision to quit. After all, it's the right thing to do, and the only way to save yourself and you loved ones a lot of grief. What isn't so easy is acting on this.

A lot of gaming addicts start out with the best intentions, but without a good plan to bolster these, nothing ever comes of them and they remain with their fingers glued to their consoles. This chapter will help you achieve an understanding of your addiction so you can turn your good intentions into a solid, effective plan that won't leave you stranded in a limbo where you are fully aware of your addiction but are unable to do anything about it.

Determine What You Like So Much About Your Games

Before anything else, you should take a moment to reflect on the nature of your love for video games, or rather what it is about them that you love so much.

Try to identify exactly what you're hooked on in your favorite game. Is there a particular series that you've been following since it first came out, eagerly awaiting each new edition? Or is it a certain genre that tickles your fancy – are all your games first-person shooter ones or high fantasy adventures? Or maybe you enjoy games that let you build your character or even the entire world from the ground up?

For me, I was hooked on Role Playing Games, such as the Final Fantasy series. I simply could not function if I did not spend hours playing the game every day. Final Fantasy offered an escape from the reality that I was facing, with an amazing storyline and characters that I felt I could identify with.

Whatever it is, pinpointing the exact details that keep you coming back for more will go a long way towards beating your gaming addiction. When you know what it is you crave, you will better be able to avoid it in the future, and can thus come up with a more effective plan for kicking the habit. As Sun Tzu said in his "Art of War," you must not only understand your enemies, but you must also understand yourself.

Identify What Triggers You to Play Like You Do

It is often the case that the games aren't the only thing to blame when addiction occurs. Aside from the fact that playing makes you a much happier person, there might be external things that drive you to seek refuge in gaming.

These external factors, or triggers, may be physical or mental cues that you were not overtly aware of when you started out. Try to pay more attention to what's happening around you and what's going on inside your head the next time you sit down to play. Do you feel the urge to play more strongly after you have a negative encounter with a certain person? Or perhaps you find that it's easier to lose yourself in the game than to think of difficult things like finances or your love life?

If you realize that something in your life is triggering you to play like you do, an important part of your plan for kicking the gaming habit will be removing that trigger from your life or finding ways to control how you respond to that factor.

Set a Date and Choose a Course of Action

The next thing on your agenda will be to set 2 dates: one on which you will start to wean yourself off video games, and another by which you aim to be game-free. Give yourself as much time as you need. Just be sure that you don't rush into it without any time to prepare, or that you don't set either date so far into the future that there is a danger of your forgetting about them.

It can help if you have them coincide with other significant dates in your life. For example, you could aim to be free of your addiction by your next birthday, the day you're set to start your new job, or even your wedding day.

Many people find it helpful to announce these dates with no small amount of fanfare. They rely on their network of friends, both in real life and in the gaming community, to remind them of what they've promised to do and to rebuke them when they fall off the proverbial wagon.

Making it public can also make it much harder for you to go back on your word. For example, set up a personal blog or write notes on Facebook that detail your journey. Then make this public, making sure all your friends and family knows. By doing so, you will have greater pressure to fulfill your goals. I personally think this is one of the most effective strategies.

If you'd rather keep your struggle with addiction to yourself, that's okay too, as long as you tell at least one person close to you so that you won't be completely alone in this fight.

After you've decided when you want to start on the road to beating video game addiction, you will have some time to think about how you want to go about it. Broadly speaking, there are two paths that you can take, and we will discuss them in the next couple of chapters.

Chapter 3 : The Slow and Steady Route

You may have reached the point when your gaming habit seems to pervade all aspects of your life. It is not uncommon for dedicated gamers to have posters and t-shirts related to their interests. People also own figurines of their favorite characters or even create recipes inspired by their game of choice. When it's reached the level that you literally find it impossible to imagine life without your game, you may want to take the slow and steady route to kicking the habit. This will help you get used to functioning without the game as a handy crutch without causing you any untoward shock that might paradoxically drive you to seek comfort in your game.

Gradually Decrease the Hours You Spend Playing

Slow and steady in this case is synonymous with simple and straightforward: the most important part of this route to beating addiction is to gradually decrease the number of hours you spend playing. Most specialists consider a gaming habit to be an addiction if you spend up to 6 hours a day at your computer or console. You should aim to whittle down this length of time bit by bit until you find yourself able to go entire days without playing.

Again, you must not give your system a nasty shock: this isn't an instance where you have to go big or go home. You don't have to cut down to a single hour of playing time on your first day.

Managing to shave 15 minutes off of your playing time each week is a significant achievement in itself. If it helps, you can think of this process as giving gaming a long, enjoyable kiss goodbye.

Be Specific About Your Goals

Once you've decided to give video games the push, there is no point in being wishy-washy about the business. While you do not have to aim high, you will have to be very specific about your goals if you wish to be successful. Setting strict but achievable goals on a weekly or daily basis will give you very little wiggle room where you will be in danger of falling back into bad habits.

For instance, meaning to take an hour off your weekly playing time is all right if you can make yourself comply with it, but if you will keep sneaking in 10 more minutes by telling yourself you'll take the entire game-free hour all in one go on the last day of the week (and you know how easily this can happen), it is very likely that you will end up missing your goal. It is thus far more efficient to reduce your daily gaming routine by a specific and manageable 5 minutes per day.

Allow Yourself the Occasional Treat

Kicking the gaming habit via the slow and steady route does not mean that you have to make yourself suffer – in fact, getting rid of your addiction with the least possible discomfort is the entire point of the process! Given this, it is acceptable to allow yourself the occasional gaming-related treat for a certain amount of good behavior.

Think of beating your video game addiction as going on a strict diet. Religious dieters will sometimes treat themselves to a multi-flavored ice cream sundae as a reward for an entire week of sticking to the program, and you can do the gaming equivalent of this as long as you are certain that you can keep it from going overboard.

So go ahead. Let yourself play an entire level of your game if you've managed to complete an entire project without once turning to your computer for procrastination and solace. Or the treat does not even have to involve actual gaming if you are not sure that you will be able to check yourself once you've got your hands on a controller. Buying yourself some gaming merchandise, like key chains and patches, is an acceptable alternative.

There is no getting around the fact that the game must have once been a huge positive force in your life before things got out of hand, especially if it helped you get through tough times, and there is nothing wrong with celebrating your love for it in small, non-destructive ways.

Chapter 4: Going Cold Turkey

It may also be the case that your dependence on video games has reached such critical levels that immediate and drastic action is called for. If things are at the point when playing causes you to skip meals, lose sleep, and neglect to bathe for several days straight, then your choice may be the option favored by many cigarette smokers and alcoholics: going cold turkey.

In this method, you will stop having anything to do with video games suddenly and all at once in the hopes of achieving a purge that will cure you of your need to play. In direct contrast to the gradual change we talked about in Chapter 3, going cold turkey is expected to come as a shock. It will not be gentle, but it can be extremely effective if you manage to pull it off.

Make It Impossible to Start Playing Again

Quitting abruptly does not mean that you quit without making preparations, however. In order for this technique to be effective, you will have to make it impossible – or at least extremely difficult – for you to start playing again.

Depending on how deeply you are addicted to video games, the measures you have to take may range from the relatively simple to the gaming equivalent of having you jump through flaming hoops.

You should actively look for ways to make it hard for you to access your games. It is, after all, called addiction for a reason, and simple willpower will not be enough to see you through. Be harsh here, and do not flinch from what you have to do. Sell your XBox 360 or PlayStation 3 or any other gadgets whose sole purpose is gaming. Delete your gaming accounts, or, if you've reached such rarefied levels that getting rid of them would be a waste, sell them to someone for whom gaming is not as much as a pitfall.

Uninstall games and related apps from your computer and smart phone, and be sure to sell or throw away the discs too. It might also be a good idea to put your gaming merchandise in storage for the time being – it might be nice to keep reminders of the good times you had with video games, but don't have them visible while you're trying to quit.

Take the Opportunity to Get Away for a While

Going cold turkey does not necessarily equate to torture. Make things a bit easier for yourself by taking the opportunity to get away for a while and timing the start of your gaming purge with a trip that will take you away from the environment where you usually play. You can start during an out-of-town conference, a road trip with friends, or your family's annual camping trip. Just make sure that you will have other things to occupy your time so that the video games you're missing won't be at the forefront of your mind.

If you think that a simple vacation won't be enough to keep you off video games for long, you may want to consider approaching groups or institutions that specialize in the treatment of gaming addiction. They may offer residential inpatient treatment for gaming addicts, where you can stay in a safe, comfortable environment that is free of any kind of games or gaming devices in the company of other people who are going through the same thing.

Being cooped up is not everyone's cup of tea, however. If it doesn't sound good to you, you might want to look into the wilderness therapy that some groups offer. These sessions can be thought of as camping trips that combine great therapy techniques and the calming, somewhat isolating effect of nature so that you can learn to cope without your games and be comfortable with yourself as a person.

I found this strategy particularly effective when I was combating my addiction. I took a trip to Yosemite with a few buddies and spent a few days there enjoying nature. We didn't have our games to distract us and simply being in the outdoors without our laptops and consoles actually helped us immensely. After going back home, I felt fresh and rejuvenated.

Chapter 5 : Staying Video Game Free for Life

Even after you've gone through the motions of giving up video games, even if you've done everything just like you're supposed to, it is still possible for you to relapse when something goes wrong later on. This chapter will point out what you need to do and what mindset you should have in order to stay video game free for life.

Go Easy on Yourself While You're Quitting

Kicking your video game addiction will need a lot of discipline and self-control on your part, whether you choose to go slow or go cold turkey, but that does not mean you have to be unduly harsh on yourself. Getting worked up over minor failings, like missing deadlines or giving in to the urge to play after you've exhausted your set time, will not help you at all. Such negativity will be extremely detrimental to what should be a healing process, especially since a large part of beating any addiction relies on raising your self-worth and your belief in your abilities.

Try to think of it like this: failing to meet some of your goals isn't a good thing, but don't beat yourself up over it. You can have a little time to mope, but you need to pick yourself up, think about how you can improve things the next time around, and move on.

Find a New Hobby
It will help a lot if you find a new hobby. Just as ex-smokers often need to find a new focus, like chewing gum or sucking on lozenges, you should channel your energy into new interests – and these interests should NOT be new video games!

There are so many activities that you could try, from quiet, individual hobbies like crocheting or art to wildly adventurous things like rock climbing or white water rafting. You can even explore interests related to the games that you used to love. If your favorite character wielded a sword, try taking up fencing! Or you could learn Latin so that you finally understand what your characters were chanting while they worked magic. Just don't be intimidated or let yourself be held back by the notion that you might not be good at something: anything can be learned as long as you put enough effort and time into it.

For me, since I also play piano, I downloaded all my favorite sheet music from my favorite games, especially Final Fantasy X, and started learning them. By doing so, I still felt connected to the game, but I was not actually not falling into the trap of playing the game.

Ask for Help If You Need It

One thing you should NOT do is try to quit on your own. Dealing with any kind of addiction is hard, and doing so without support from anyone will only make your struggle worse. If you need help, ask your friends and family for it: you will not be doing your loved ones any favors by keeping them in the dark. Their understanding and encouragement may very well be what reminds you to steer clear of gaming in the future.

You may also have to face the reality of having to seek professional aid with your video game addiction if you can't manage it on your own, or if your loved ones, though supportive, don't know where to start when it comes to getting you clean. Going to a therapist, psychiatrist, or psychologist is nothing to be ashamed about if that's what helps you finally beat your addiction for good.

Learn to Avoid and Deal with Your Triggers

In order to put an end your video game addiction once and for all, you will also have to address the triggers that drove you to play so obsessively in the first place. The best course of action would be to avoid them before they make you relapse or drive you to worse things than the simple need to play. Don't be afraid to leave toxic relationships, even if it means breaking up with a partner or loving a relative from a distance instead of constantly exposing yourself to someone who makes you so unhappy. And you similarly must not be afraid to walk away from situations that can drive you back to gaming as a form of escapism. Your job or your school is simply not worth sacrificing your sanity and well-being.

Conclusion

Thank you again for downloading this book!

I really hope this book was able to help you figure out ways to combat your video game addiction.

If you enjoyed this book, please take the time to share your thoughts and post a review on Amazon. It'd be greatly appreciated!

I'd also love to hear your feedback on how I can improve this book!

Thank you and good luck!

Printed in Great Britain
by Amazon